W9-BXO-091

FAR-OUT and UNUSUAL pets

# Hermit Crabs Cool Pets!

Alvin and Virginia Silverstein and Laura Silverstein Nunn

**Enslow Elementary**
an imprint of

**Enslow Publishers, Inc.**
40 Industrial Road
Box 398
Berkeley Heights, NJ 07922
USA
http://www.enslow.com

Enslow Elementary, an imprint of Enslow Publishers, Inc.

Enslow Elementary® is a registered trademark of Enslow Publishers, Inc.



**Library of Congress Cataloging-in-Publication Data**

Silverstein, Alvin.
Hermit crabs : cool pets! / by Alvin Silverstein, Virginia Silverstein, and Laura Silverstein Nunn.
p. cm. — (Far-out and unusual pets)
Includes bibliographical references and index.
Summary: "Provides basic information about hermit crabs and keeping them as pets"—Provided by publisher.
ISBN 978-0-7660-3684-0
1. Hermit crabs as pets—Juvenile literature. I. Silverstein, Virginia B. II. Nunn, Laura Silverstein. III. Title.
SF459.H47S55 2012
639'.67—dc22 2009043924

Printed in the United States of America

102010 Lake Book Manufacturing, Inc., Melrose Park, IL

10 9 8 7 6 5 4 3 2 1

**To Our Readers:** We have done our best to make sure all Internet Addresses in this book were active and appropriate when we went to press. However, the author and the publisher have no control over and assume no liability for the material available on those Internet sites or on other Web sites they may link to. Any comments or suggestions can be sent by e-mail to comments@enslow.com or to the address on the back cover.

♻ Enslow Publishers, Inc., is committed to printing our books on recycled paper. The paper in every book contains 10% to 30% post-consumer waste (PCW). The cover board on the outside of each book contains 100% PCW. Our goal is to do our part to help young people and the environment too!

**Photo Credits:** Alex Mustard/Photo Researchers, Inc., p. 6; Associated Press, pp. 28, 36; © Carles Zamorano Cabello/Alamy, pp. 15, 18; Courtesy Kirk Weick/The Hermit Crab Patch, p. 14; Crabzilla, p. 42; Craig Cook, p. 43; Dorling Kindersley/Getty Images, p. 19; © IndexStock/SuperStock, p. 34 (bottom); iStockphoto.com: © Andrew Brigmond, p. 34 (top), © Deborah Maxemow, p. 12, © Juliana Halvorson, p. 4, © Kyle Eertmoed, p. 44, © Thomas Maher, p. 10; Josh Schulz, p. 22; © Malcolm Schuyl/Alamy, p. 20; © Mark Eveleigh/Alamy, p. 31; Renee Parilak, p. 33; Richard Hutchings/Photolibrary, p. 8; Sarah Vessels, p. 25; Shutterstock.com, pp. 3, 13 (top and bottom), 17, 27, 30, 34 (left).

**Illustration Credits:** © 2010 Gerald Kelley, www.geraldkelley.com

**Cover Photo:** Shutterstock.com

# Contents

Hermit crabs don't grow their own shells. They use shells from other animals, such as snails.

# 1

# Life in a Borrowed Shell

How would you like a pet that carries its home on its back? No, it's not a turtle. It's a hermit crab. Hermit crabs, like turtles, need their hard, outer shell to protect themselves from danger. But hermit crabs don't grow their own shells—they borrow them. They usually live in empty snail shells. When a hermit crab gets too big for its shell, it looks for a new one.

Hermit crabs are popular pets because they are cheap, easy to care for, and cute. They may not be as cuddly as a dog or cat, but having a pet hermit crab can be lots of fun. You can watch the crab

marine (sea) hermit crab

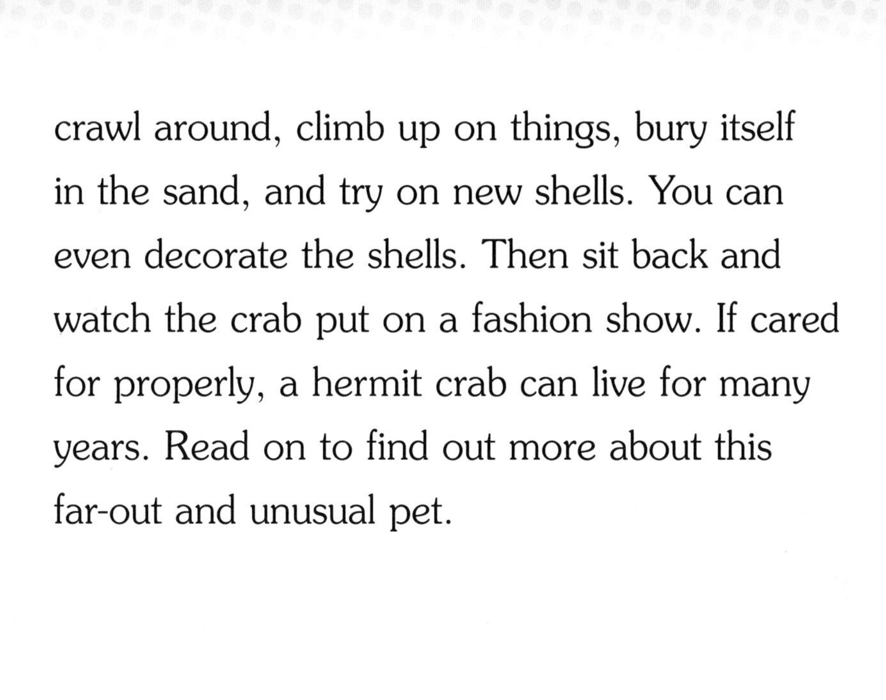

crawl around, climb up on things, bury itself in the sand, and try on new shells. You can even decorate the shells. Then sit back and watch the crab put on a fashion show. If cared for properly, a hermit crab can live for many years. Read on to find out more about this far-out and unusual pet.

Far Out!

## Land or Sea?

**Most hermit crabs live in the sea. Some kinds live on land, though. They return to the sea only to mate and lay their eggs. These land hermit crabs are the ones that are kept as pets.**

Hermit crabs make great pets for responsible owners.

# 2

# The World of Land Hermit Crabs

When you think of a crab, you probably picture one with a flat body moving sideways along the seashore. This isn't a hermit crab. Hermit crabs are distant relatives of the common shore crab. You may see hermit crabs living around bays and tide pools near the ocean. You can also find them for sale in pet stores and boardwalk gift shops.

## Wild Ways

A hermit crab is not your usual pet. Take its looks, for example. Its eyes aren't even part of its face! They sit at the end of tube-shaped eye stalks.

In the wild, hermit crabs are usually found around tide pools.

The crab also has a *lot* of legs—ten of them! The front pair are big, strong claws. The small, back legs hold tightly to the inside of the shell. A hermit crab also has some tiny "legs" around its mouth. It uses those as grabbers to hold and tear its food.

A hermit crab is not soft and furry like a cat or a dog. Its "skin" is a tough outer covering. It is called an exoskeleton, which means "skeleton on the outside." Some animals, including dogs and cats, have a skeleton inside their body. But crabs, insects, and many other animals have their skeletons on the outside. In addition, the hermit crab wears a shell like a suit of armor that covers most of its body. This is usually a hard, spiral shell. The crab's body curls up inside the shell.

But it's not just looks that make a hermit crab an interesting pet. If you watch one for awhile, you will see it do some fascinating things. Even though it now lives in your home, it still keeps its wild ways. The hermit crab acts just as it would if it were actually living in the wild.

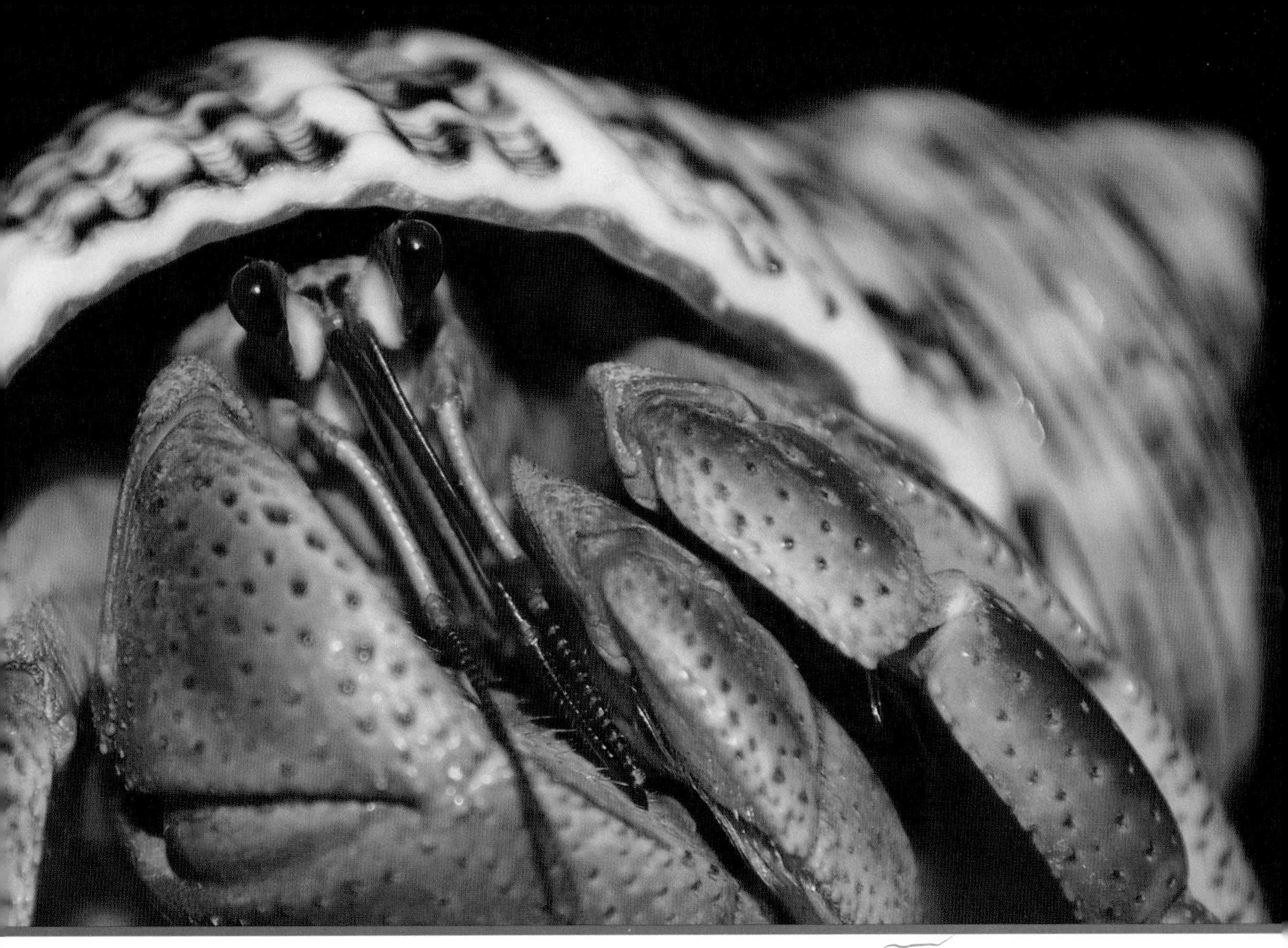

A hermit crab's eyes are attached to eye stalks.

## Wet and Wild

Land hermit crabs live in warm, moist places. They are usually found along the coast in tropical regions, such as the Florida Keys, Venezuela, Tahiti, and Australia. They live on sandy beaches or in the nearby forests.

A hermit crab in its borrowed shell (right) looks quite different from an ordinary crab on the beach, such as the one shown below.

Far Out!

## Walk This Way

**Most kinds of crabs usually move sideways, but hermit crabs walk forward.**

Although land hermit crabs spend most of their time out of the ocean, they breathe through gills. Gills are organs for breathing. Our lungs take in oxygen from the air we breathe. Gills get oxygen out of water. Fish, lobsters, and many other water

This is what a hermit crab looks like out of its shell. Notice the tiny gills.

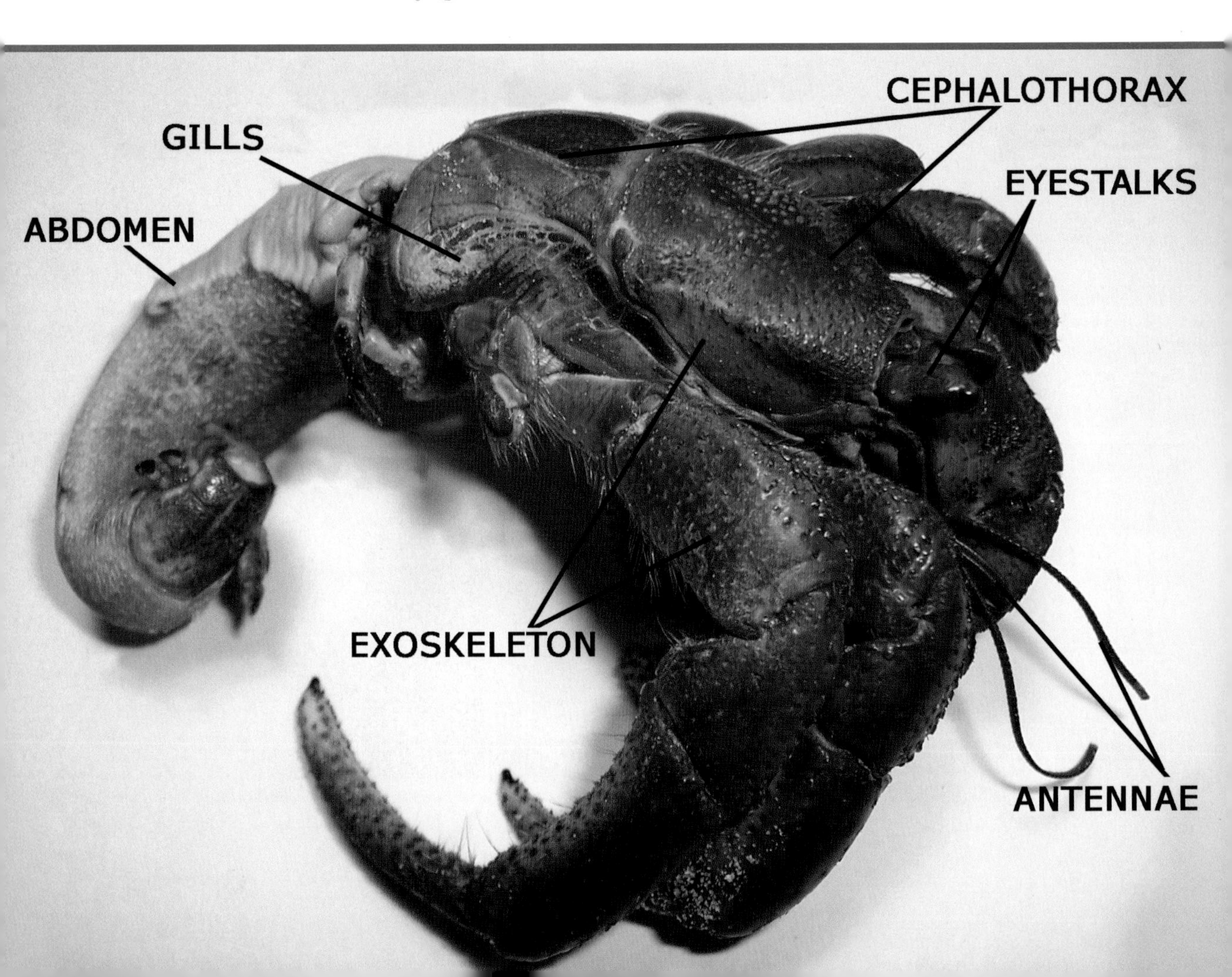

Some wild hermit crabs like to climb trees, so your pet hermit crab may climb your furniture!

Far Out!

## Tree Crabs

Some kinds of land hermit crabs are expert climbers. They are sometimes called "tree crabs." They use their sharp front claws and their walking legs to go up a tree. In the wild, these crabs will climb trees and snack on fruit, leaves, or bark.

When hermit crabs are kept as pets, they climb up and over whatever is in their way. They will even climb on the furniture. But they could hurt themselves if they fall.

animals breathe with gills. So do hermit crabs, whether they live in the ocean or on the land.

Even though they have gills, land hermit crabs cannot live underwater. Their gills are small and can take in oxygen from air. If these crabs stayed underwater too long, they would drown. (The hermit crabs that live in the sea have larger gills that work only in water.)

Gills don't work unless they are moist. If they dry out, the crab will die. In the wild, land hermit crabs spend their days out of the hot sun. They hide in places where it is cool and moist—in shallow burrows or underneath rocks, leaves, and fallen branches.

Hermit crabs carry a supply of water inside their shell. This extra water helps keep their gills moist while they rest. It also comes in handy when they wander away from the shore. The crabs may travel a mile or two to look for food. However, they have to return to the water from time to time. They may soak for awhile and refill their water supply.

These hermit crabs hide
on the side of a rock.

## Suit of Armor

A hermit crab's borrowed shell serves as both a house and a suit of armor. Its banana-shaped body can twist into an empty snail shell for a perfect fit. The crab takes the shell along with it wherever it goes. The soft, rear part of its body stays inside the shell at all times.

Just like any other shell-wearing creature, the hermit crab uses its shell for protection against predators—animals that want to eat it. When a strange animal gets too close, the crab pulls the rest of its body into its shell and hides inside. Its large, front claw covers the opening like a trap door.

Hermit crabs can hide in their shells.

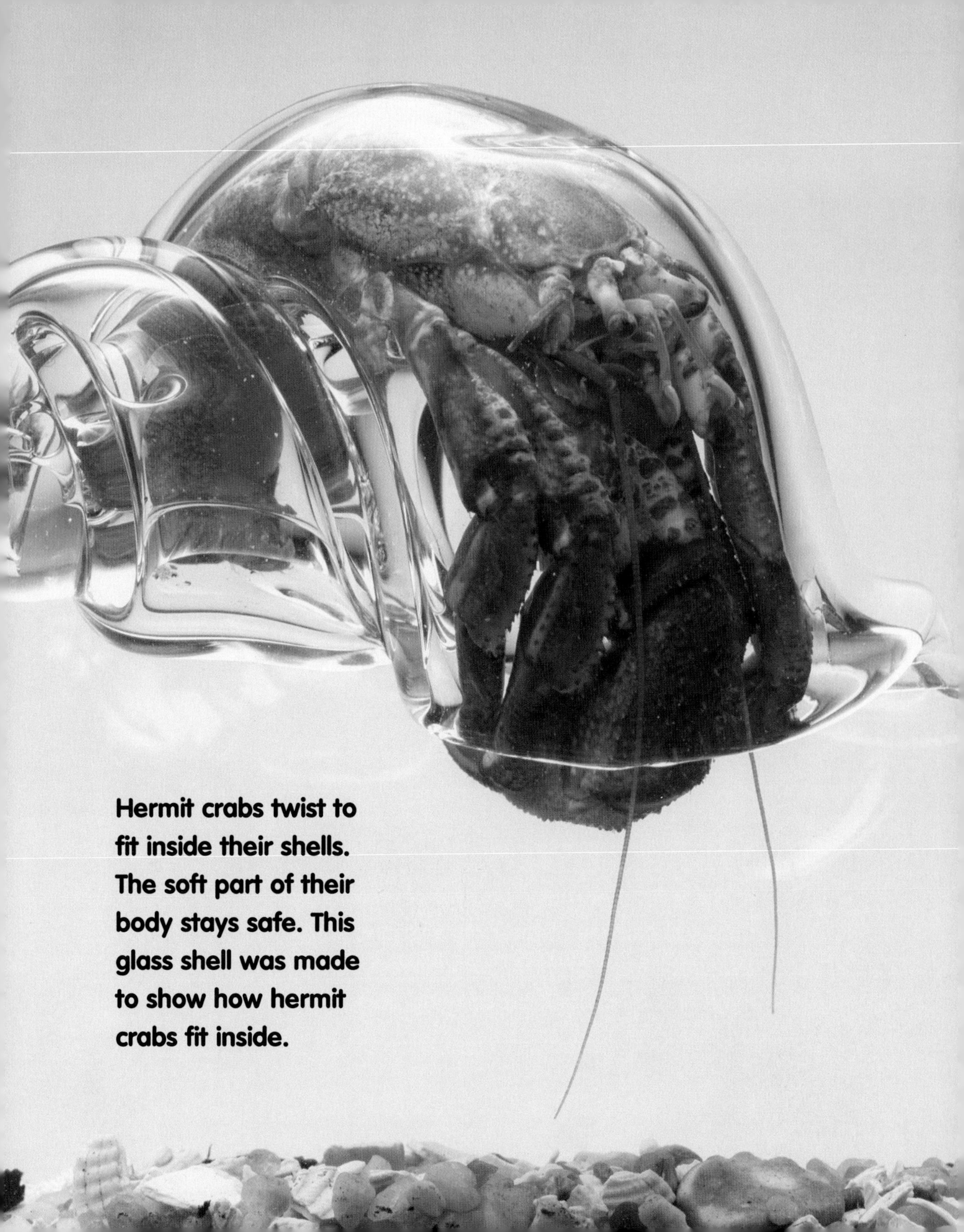

**Hermit crabs twist to fit inside their shells. The soft part of their body stays safe. This glass shell was made to show how hermit crabs fit inside.**

Far Out!

## Whatever Works

**In the wild, a hermit crab that can't find an empty snail shell of the right size and shape will use whatever's around. Sometimes you might even find a hermit crab carrying part of a bottle, a broken light bulb, or some other trash on its back!**

# 3

# It's Changing Time!

What do you do when you've outgrown your clothes? Your shirt is too tight and your pant legs are way above your ankles. It's time to buy new clothes that fit you better, right? When a hermit crab grows, its outer covering—the exoskeleton—gets too tight for its body. It has to shed its exoskeleton. This is called molting. Underneath is a fresh new covering that gives the crab more room to grow. But now the hermit crab is too big for its old shell. It needs to find a new, larger one.

This hermit crab has just molted. Its old exoskeleton is on the right.

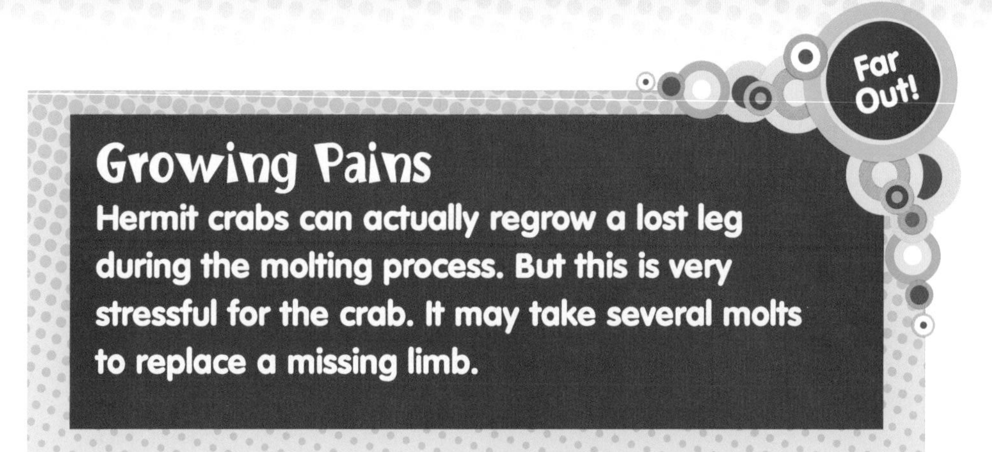

Far Out!
Growing Pains
Hermit crabs can actually regrow a lost leg during the molting process. But this is very stressful for the crab. It may take several molts to replace a missing limb.


## Out With the Old, In With the New

All hermit crabs molt as their bodies grow. Large crabs molt every twelve to eighteen months. Smaller ones molt more often.

Hermit crabs normally hang out with other hermit crabs. But when it is time to molt, they would rather be alone. First, the crab looks for a safe hideaway. It may dig down in the sand, under leaves, or in a burrow. Then the old exoskeleton cracks open down the back. The crab wriggles out of it. A new exoskeleton has grown under the old one. It is soft and moist, at first. The shell acts as a mold for the crab's soft body. The crab eats the old exoskeleton. This gives it minerals to help build up its new exoskeleton.

It may take weeks for the new outer covering to get thick and strong. During this time, the crab is very weak. It must hide until its *exoskeleton* hardens. Otherwise the crab could be hurt or eaten by other animals—even other hermit crabs!

## The Search Is On

Now that the hermit crab is larger, it finds that its old shell is too tight. So it has to start looking for a bigger one. When a hermit crab finds an empty snail shell, it checks it carefully. It rolls the shell over and runs its claws

## Hermit Crabs Without Shells?

Hermit crabs didn't always wear shells. Long ago, marine hermit crabs (those that lived in the sea) protected their soft bodies by hiding out between rocks along the coast. Coming out to look for food was risky, though. They had no protection against predators. Sometimes they found shells from snails that had died. These shells were good places to hide. Some of the hermit crabs began carrying the best shells around with them. That way, they could move safely while looking for food. In some parts of the world, marine hermit crabs still live in rock holes.

Shell-changing happens very quickly, so the crab stays safe.

over the inside and outside. It may try the shell on for size. If the crab doesn't like the way it feels, it will return to its old home and continue its search.

A hermit crab may try on several shells until it finds one that fits just right. Then the crab will leave the old, outgrown shell and slip backward into its new home.

Hermit crabs sometimes fight each other for shells. By tapping each other with their legs and claws, one crab will try to force the other away

These hermit crabs are fighting. One wants the other's shell.

from the shell they both want. Sometimes a crab will try to fight for a shell that already has another crab in it! It uses its legs and claws to rock the shell back and forth, occasionally jabbing the crab inside the shell. Eventually, the victim may be forced out of its shell, and the attacker moves in.

It is important to learn how to properly house and handle your new pet.

# 4

# Caring for Your Crab

Hermit crabs can become a part of the family. And just like any pet, hermit crabs have different personalities. Some are curious and quickly poke their heads out of their shells. Some are friendly and crawl on your hand. Others are shy. They hide in their shells, and it's hard to get them to come out. Some are easily upset and may give you a painful pinch with a claw. Getting to know your hermit crab can be a really interesting experience.

## Getting Your Own Hermit Crab

Where do you get your very own hermit crab? You can buy them in many pet stores and seaside gift shops. Hermit crabs can vary greatly in size, from just three centimeters (a little more than an inch) to more than fifteen centimeters (six inches) long. The purple claw crab is the most commonly sold. Its name comes from the fact that it does indeed have a large purple claw.

In the wild, hermit crabs live in large groups. There can be as many as one hundred of them! They crawl over one another and rest together in huge piles. So it is a good idea to buy two or more hermit crabs as pets. Having company will make life in a tank seem more like their home in the wild. It is also fun to watch how several crabs get along with each other. The hermit crabs you keep together should be close in size. Larger hermit crabs might eat smaller ones.

Purple claw crabs are very popular as pets.

Wild hermit crabs like to live in groups. You may want to buy your pet a friend.

Far Out!

### Talk to Me

**Hermit crabs may "talk" to each other by tapping each other's shells with their claws. They may also make strange chirping noises. This can happen when they are hurt or upset.**

You don't have to worry about your hermit crabs having babies, even if you have pets of both sexes. They need to be in seawater to mate and have babies.

## Setting Up Your Crab's Home

How can you make your pet hermit crab feel at home? The best thing to do is to make its new home as close as possible to its living conditions in nature. Use a 10-gallon tank if you have only one crab. If you are keeping two or more crabs, you will need a larger tank. Keep a tight-fitting cover over the tank. Hermit crabs are known escape artists. They will climb up the sides and try to get out of the tank.

Since land hermit crabs in the wild live in warm, moist places, their tank should be warm and moist, as well. It should have a heater that keeps the temperature in the range of 21 to 29°C (70 to 85°F). Mist your crabs and their tank with lukewarm water to keep them from drying out.

Put a few inches of sand or dirt on the bottom of the tank. It should be deep enough for the

A properly prepared "crabitat" will keep your new pet happy and healthy.

## Colorful Shells

**Would you like to see your hermit crab wearing shells with cool colors? You can actually color the shells yourself. But you must use only vegetable dyes made for coloring foods. The crabs often handle empty shells and climb onto the shells of other hermit crabs. Nail polish, paints, or crayons might contain poisonous chemicals. Handling them or nibbling on them could make your pet sick.**

hermit crab to dig burrows and hide, especially during molting. Include rocks and sticks for the crab to climb on and hide under and a good selection of shells. You can buy shells of different sizes in a pet store or pick them up at the beach.

## Getting to Know Your Crab

Picking up a hermit crab for the first time may be painful. No, it won't bite you. But if you're not careful, it will clamp its claw onto your finger and hold on. Ouch! Don't try to yank it off—that might hurt your pet. Just put the crab under running lukewarm water, and it will let go.

When you pick up a hermit crab, hold it by the top or back of its shell. Keep your other hand flat.

Hold your hermit crab often so that it gets used to you and will not be afraid to be picked up.

Set the crab down on your flat hand to avoid getting pinched. Make sure there is a surface close by so it won't get hurt if it falls. Crabs that are handled often will get used to people and are less likely to hurt you. Eventually, you might be able to teach your hermit crab to eat from your hand.

Your hermit crab's tank will be its home, but it will also enjoy roaming around the house. Exploring a living room or a bedroom is good exercise. Be sure to keep an eye on your crab, though, when you take it out to play.

Even though hermit crabs are expert climbers, they are clumsy. In the wild, they often fall out of trees. While roaming in a house, they can easily tumble off tables, beds, and other high places. They can also get lost under a couch or in a closet.

Don't let your pet stay out of its tank too long. Unless you live in a tropical climate, the air in your house will be too cool and dry for a hermit crab. Remember that it needs to stay moist to survive.

Far Out!

## The Night Life

**Do you get to stay up late? If you don't, you may have trouble sleeping with a hermit crab in your bedroom. Hermit crabs are most active at night. In fact, they may keep you up at night making scratching or chirping noises. So you may want to think twice about keeping a hermit crab tank in your bedroom.**

## Don't Bother Me, I'm Molting!

If you notice that your hermit crab is not eating, is not very active, and stays in one place, don't worry. It may look dead, but it's probably getting ready to molt. The crab may stay buried in the sand at the bottom of the tank for up to two weeks before molting. Then the molting process may take a few more weeks. So be patient. Make sure the crab has a variety of new shells to choose from for its new, bigger self.

If you have more than one pet hermit crab, the molting crab should be taken to a special tank where it can be alone. Remember, molting leaves the crab weak and helpless. It can't protect itself if another crab tries to harm it.

If you set up the molting tank with dirt piled up high at one end, the hermit crab may dig down right next to the glass wall. Then you can watch it molt.

## Feeding Time

What do you feed a hermit crab? Pet stores sell special hermit crab food. You can buy bags of pellets or cans of food. (You may need to break up or crush the pellets for small crabs.) These pet foods provide a healthy diet. You should also feed your crab fresh fruits, such as pieces of apples, bananas, pears, and grapes. Vegetables, including romaine lettuce, cabbage, carrots, and broccoli, are great treats, too. Hermit crabs will also eat grains, such as crackers and cereal.

You can feed your hermit crab fresh fruits and vegetables.

A hermit crab's water dishes should be shallow, so the crab can climb in and out.

Hermit crabs also need a source of calcium. This chemical helps make their exoskeleton strong. (We need calcium to keep our bones strong, too.) Crushed oyster shells and cuttlebones are good calcium foods you can buy in a pet store. You can also give your crabs crushed eggshells. (Boil them to kill any germs.)

**Calcium makes a hermit crab's exoskeleton strong.**

You will soon learn how much your pet crab will eat each day. Throw out any leftovers. If you leave them in the tank, they may spoil or get moldy.

Hermit crabs need a dish of drinking water. They may also like a dish of salt water to climb into and soak for awhile. The dishes should be shallow, though, to prevent drowning. Pet stores sell feeding and water dishes shaped like seashells. You can also use clamshells or other flat shells you find at the beach.

* * *

Hermit crabs don't cost much, but they can provide lots of fun. Owning pet hermit crabs is a big responsibility, though. With good care, they can live for a really long time—up to twenty years or more!

# Words to Know

**abdomen**—The hind part of the body of animals, such as insects, spiders, and crabs.

**antennae**—Feelers; a pair of movable organs on the head of insects and crustaceans (such as crabs and lobsters); typically used for smell and taste.

**calcium**—A chemical found in bones, shells, and many rocks.

**cephalothorax (*pronounced* SEF-uh-loh-THOR-ax)**—A combination of the animal's head and the front part of the body.

**exoskeleton**—The hard outer shell or covering of many animals.

**gills**—Breathing organs that take in oxygen from water. Fish, crabs, and other water animals have gills instead of lungs.

**marine hermit crab**—A kind of hermit crab that lives in the ocean or saltwater pools throughout its life.

**molt**—The periodic shedding of an animal's hair, skin, or feathers.

**organ**—A body structure specialized for a particular job or jobs.

**oxygen**—A gas that makes up about 21 percent of the air we breathe. Animals and plants can't live without a supply of oxygen.

**predator**—An animal that hunts and kills other animals for food.

# Learn More

## Books

De Vosjoli, Philippe. *Land Hermit Crabs*. Laguna Hills, Calif.: Advanced Vivarium Systems, 2005.

Edina, Kelly Doudna. *Hidden Hermit Crabs*. Minneapolis: ABDO Pub. Co., 2007.

Pavia, Audrey. *Hermit Crab*. Hoboken, N.J.: Wiley Publishing, Inc., 2006.

Weber, Valerie J. *Why Animals Live in Shells*. Pleasantville, N.Y.: Weekly Reader Books, 2008.

## Web Sites

**The Crab Street Journal.**

<http://www.crabstreetjournal.com>

*This is an online magazine, featuring articles written by land hermit crab owners. Articles include information on hermit crab biology, pet care tips, stories, contests, and links to other hermit crab sites.*

**Hermit-Crabs.com.**

<http://hermit-crabs.com/>

*In this site, a longtime hermit crab owner provides information about owning hermit crabs, including links to basic care, crab behavior, FAQ page, advice on picking shells, and lots of great photos.*

**HermitCrabs.org.**

<http://www.hermitcrabs.org/>

*This site gives the basics on hermit crabs and their care, illustrated with vivid, color photos.*

# Index